AF228654

# What Polar Bears Do

Katie Peters

GRL Consultant Diane Craig,
Certified Literacy Specialist

Lerner Publications ◆ Minneapolis

Lerner Publications
An imprint of Lerner Publishing Group, Inc.
241 First Avenue North
Minneapolis, MN 55401 USA

For reading levels and more information, look up this title at www.lernerbooks.com.

Main body text set in Memphis Pro 24/39
Typeface provided by Linotype.

Photo Acknowledgments
The images in this book are used with the permission of: © Alexey Seafarer/Shutterstock Images,
p. 3; © FloridaStock/Shutterstock Images, pp. 4–5, 6–7, 16 (left); © Caleb Foster/Shutterstock
Images, pp. 8–9, 16 (right); © GTW/Shutterstock Images, pp. 10–11; © AndreAnita/iStockphoto,
pp. 12–13, 16 (center); © SergeyKlopotov/Shutterstock Images, pp. 14–15.

Front cover: © FloridaStock/Shutterstock Images

**Library of Congress Cataloging-in-Publication Data**

Names: Peters, Katie, author.
Title: What Polar bears do / Katie Peters.
Description: Minneapolis : Lerner Publications, [2025] | Series: Let's look at polar animals
    (pull ahead readers - nonfiction) | Includes index. | Audience: Ages 4–7 | Audience:
    Grades K–1 | Summary: "Polar bears know how to survive in their polar environments.
    Leveled text and exciting photographs help young readers learn about how these bears
    live in the cold. Pairs with the fiction title, Polar Bear Lessons"—Provided by publisher.
Identifiers: LCCN 2023031598 (print) | LCCN 2023031599 (ebook) | ISBN 9798765626313
    (library binding) | ISBN 9798765629352 (paperback) | ISBN 9798765634806 (epub)
Subjects: LCSH: Polar bear—Juvenile literature.
Classification: LCC QL737.C27 P423 2024  (print) | LCC QL737.C27  (ebook) | DDC 599.786—
    dc23/eng/20230717

LC record available at https://lccn.loc.gov/2023031598
LC ebook record available at https://lccn.loc.gov/2023031599

Manufactured in the United States of America
1 – CG – 7/15/24

# Table of Contents

What Polar Bears Do

Polar bears live on the ice.

Polar bears hunt on the ice.

Polar bears hunt in
the water too.

Polar bears hunt for seals.

Polar bears dig dens
in the snow.

Polar bears sleep in their dens.

# Did You See It?

ice

snow

water

# Index